This book belongs to:

____

www.ingramcontent.com/pod-product-compliance
Lightning Source LLC
Chambersburg PA
CBHW070804220526
45466CB00002B/537
9781694644725